THE
DREAM
JOURNAL

Guided by the Words of
Dr. Martin Luther King Jr.

**MartinLuther
KingJr.***Library*

HarperCollins books may be purchased for educational, business, or sales promotional use. For information, please email the Special Markets Department at SPsales@harpercollins.com.

FIRST EDITION

Designed by SBI Book Arts, LLC
Background pattern by Alexvectors/Shutterstock

Library of Congress Cataloging-in-Publication Data has been applied for.

ISBN 978-0-06-323699-8

22 23 24 25 26   LSC   10 9 8 7 6 5 4 3 2 1

This journal belongs to me.

_____

Introduction

Dreaming for Yourself and for the World

Dear dream explorer, welcome to a dream journal guided by the inspiration, strength, and vision of Dr. Martin Luther King Jr., drawing on his historic speech "I Have a Dream" and other texts. In these pages you will encounter beautiful quotes from Dr. King to meditate on and questions that will help guide you to cast your contemplative gaze inward at yourself and outward at your world, as well as move you to action.

The journal is divided into three parts. PART I: PERSONAL TRANSFORMATION will lead you to self-reflect and align with your individual desires, strengths, and dreams in your quest for personal improvement. PART II: SOCIAL TRANS-FORMATION will cast your eyes on your local and global community and the social issues that may have an impact on it and will challenge you to envision healthier, happier, more equitable possibilities. Then, in the spirit of Martin Luther King Jr.'s great work, which showed the unbreakable ties between personal and social issues, struggles, and achievements, PART III: PERSONAL TRANSFORMATION MEETS SOCIAL TRANSFORMATION will guide you to see your personal dreams and your social dreams as one unified effort and will inspire you to influence yourself and your world for the better.

Each part will follow a transformational arc with four stages:

1. **THE DREAM**—A vision or dream you wish to pursue

2. **THE STRUGGLE**—A recognition of the obstacles standing in your or society's way to accomplishing THE DREAM

3. **THE POWER**—An acknowledgment of the inner and outer resources needed to overcome THE STRUGGLE

4. **THE PATH**—A statement of the steps you can take to harness THE POWER to reach your goal

There is no one right way to use this journal. You may choose to complete the first section fully before moving on to the next, dedicating yourself to consider one focused aspect of the whole at a time. You could also opt to consider THE DREAM for Parts I, II, and III first, then THE STRUGGLE, and so forth, to keep the personal-social bond at the top of your mind all the way through. Trust, dear dream explorer, that your way is the best way and will provoke valuable inner thought and outer dialogue, providing a jumping-off point to incorporate the words, thoughts, and dreams of Martin Luther King Jr. into your daily life and actions.

Go forth, dream, and put those dreams into action.

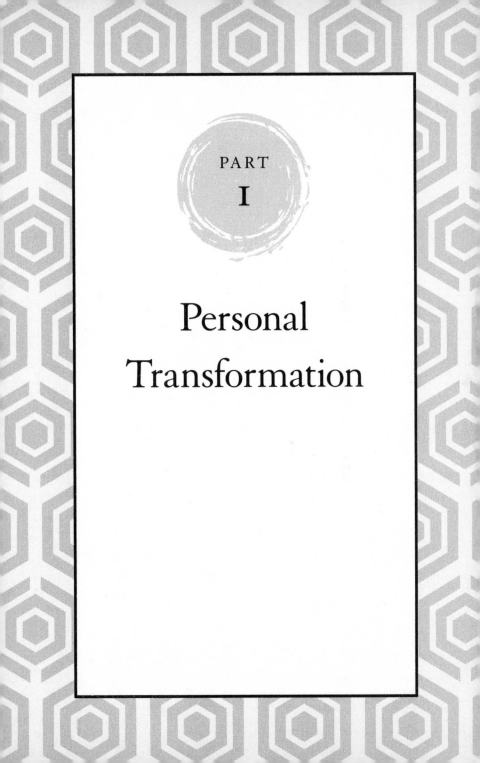

PART
I

Personal
Transformation

This section invites you to look inward. It is about personal transformation, and it invites you to discover what the unique meaning of such transformation is for you. Not only can you identify the dreams you hold, but you can name the unique qualities, talents, and resources you possess or can access that will help you achieve those dreams. No dream is too big or too small for you to tackle here. Be honest, open, and kind with yourself as you explore whatever emerges through your writing in this section of the journal.

THE
Dream

"So I say to you, my friends, that even though we must face the difficulties of today and tomorrow, I still have a dream."

Write down what your
dreams are about, the
things you would like
to accomplish in your
personal life. List these
without any limitation,
fear, or boundaries, no
matter how small or
large, how realistic or
unfeasible you may feel
them to be.

"You will change your mind; You will change your looks; You will change your smile, laugh, and ways, but no matter what you change, you will always be you."

Any dream is possible—
the first step in believing
this is to believe in
yourself. To love yourself
fully. To trust that
your visions and values
are genuine and valid.
To walk through life
with self-assurance and
confidence. Write down
which qualities you love
about yourself. What
values do you have that
you wish to remain
consistent in your life?
What parts of yourself
do you wish to grow and
foster? What aspects of
your identity do you wish
to explore more?

THE
Struggle

"No person has
the right to
rain on your
dreams."

Write down what you
feel has been limiting
you from accomplishing
your dreams. Be honest
and personal about
these limitations, with
an eye toward how you
might address them to
remove such limitations
going forward. Some of
these may be personal
challenges that may be
holding you back; others
may be larger societal
issues or pressures that
have a bearing on you
personally. Feel free to
explore these as broadly
as you wish, always
keeping in mind your
own personal goals and
wishes.

THE
Power

"We cannot walk alone."

Write down the names of people, groups, or organizations that you can trust. Whom can you confide in and be supported by? In what ways do you want to develop your network, people who will stick by your side and cheer you on as you strive after your dreams?

_____

_____

_____

_____

_____

_____

_____

_____

In what ways can you see
yourself be free of the
limitations? What values,
experiences, and people
do you think remain
essential to your life,
and what do you believe
requires new boundaries,
definitions, and distance
in order to accomplish the
things you deserve?

_____

_____

_____

_____

_____

_____

_____

_____

_____

_____

THE
Path

"Take the first step
in faith. You don't
have to see the whole
staircase, just take
the first step."

Think about the first
steps you would like to
take in order to achieve
the dreams you have
for yourself. From what
aspects of your life do you
seek liberation, change,
and resolution? How can
you harness the resources
in your life—the people,
the support systems, the
experiences, and the
values that you reflected
on earlier—to begin your
journey toward your
dreams and goals?

"If I cannot do great things, I can do small things in a great way."

When reading the works of heroes like Martin Luther King Jr., we often find ourselves looking at their biggest accomplishments and feeling overwhelmed. We think to ourselves, *How can I possibly achieve such great things? What if my dreams are too small and unimportant? What if my dreams are too big?* Though it can be daunting, the willingness and courage to dream, the revolutionary choice of dreaming, can even begin with the minutest of goals.

Write down small things you can pursue and achieve that will have an impact on your overall well-being and lead to positive change in your life.

Now write down how
they align with the larger
goals and values you have
in your life.

Now make a list of how
you can pursue them
with equal intention
and drive.

Social
Transformation

In this section, turn your gaze on the world around you—the people you see every day, those who hold public office and wield power, the systems that operate and shape the way things are. You will investigate how these things came to be, and you will ask yourself what you believe is serving individuals and society at large, and what could be improved.

THE
Dream

"I have a dream that one day every valley shall be exalted, and every hill and mountain shall be made low, the rough places will be made plain, and the crooked places will be made straight; 'and the glory of the Lord shall be revealed and all flesh shall see it together.'"

Describe what you see as an equitable society, where everyone has what they need, and no one is disparaged for a particular identity, skin color, ability, or religion. How does that imagined society compare to the one you inhabit today? What are your dreams for your community, your state, your nation, the world? List these without any limitation, fear, or boundaries, no matter how small or large, how realistic or unfeasible you may feel them to be.

THE
Struggle

"We are not makers of history. We are made by history."

When thinking about our dreams and aspirations for our communities and society at large, it is also important to reflect on what has shaped them over the years. Do you know the history of the town, city, or country you live in, especially as it relates to the goals you have for your community, and could you describe these details here? Perhaps explore what factors have made things the way they are today, or what customs, people, experiences, and values have developed into the place you inhabit, for better or worse. Do you see any of these factors and entities standing in the way of positive change? How and why?

"Hate is too great a

burden to bear."

Martin Luther King Jr. was always poised when he had to be: facing his congregation, his followers, and the public. One can only imagine the range of emotions that emerged for King as he led the fight for racial justice. But he understood that allowing anger and hatred to fester would have a negative impact on himself, those closest to him, and the struggle for freedom, so he channeled that energy as best he could into his work, spurring him to write "Letter from Birmingham Jail," for example. Here, write about an issue facing you or others that spurs you to action. What emerges for you as you ponder the situations that King found himself in? What's that like for you? The anger of justice denied is completely normal. Sit with it as long as you need to. Ultimately, naming it will help you harness it rather than let it control you.

THE
Power

"Our powerful weapons
are the voices, the feet,
and the bodies of dedicated,
united people, moving
without rest toward
a just goal."

Martin Luther King Jr. knew that power lies with the people. Unified behind a common passion and goal, and by combating injustice, those wishing for a better world were numerous and unstoppable. Consider the passions and values you wish to share with others, and write down how you imagine yourself expressing them. Who are some members of your community or organizations who are also working toward your dreams or intersecting ones? Think about how you could partner with these individuals or groups to generate people power toward your common goals.

THE
Path

"We must use time creatively, and forever realize that the time is always ripe to do right."

It can be all too easy at times to defer pursuing your dreams for your community and society. There is work, family, friends, the nonstop rhythm of daily life—and then the challenges of building people power with varying schedules and commitments. And it can be overwhelming to face the looming issues in the world around you and find the strength to do something. Nevertheless, taking on the pressing needs of your people around you, even in small ways, can help you regain a sense of agency and strength and can even inspire you to go bigger. You may even find the relationships you build and the connections you make nourishing and invigorating as you proceed on your path. Write down ways in which you can make time out of your day to work toward your dreams. What does that time look like for you? Is it volunteering at a local organization? Is it gathering with friends to educate yourselves on an issue you care about and bringing that knowledge to your community? Is it getting involved in local politics, canvasing your area, and finding out what your neighbors' needs are? Give yourself the space to think about time and how you can use it creatively to embrace your pursuits and dreams.

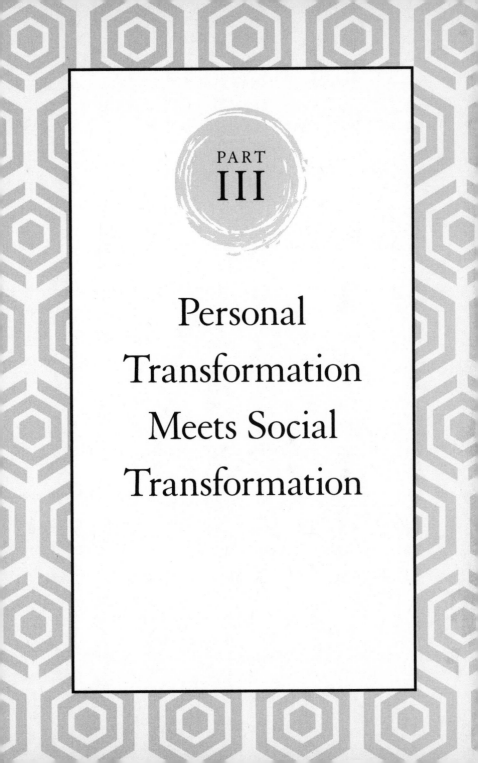

PART
III

Personal
Transformation
Meets Social
Transformation

In "I Have a Dream," Martin Luther King Jr. cited the Declaration of Independence, which expresses that we are all created equal and have the right to pursue our own happiness. He noted that people from all walks of life had joined in the struggle for civil rights, regardless of how directly or indirectly it affected them. "No one is free until we are all free," he famously said, inextricably merging our personal liberty with the liberty of everyone on this earth. We all suffer when justice is for one and not for all. In this section, you can explore how, why, and where your personal dreams meet your dreams for both your local and global communities, and go through the steps to imagine a way forward to freedom for all.

THE
Dream

"Love is somehow the key that unlocks the door which leads to ultimate reality."

One of the most consistent themes in Martin Luther King Jr.'s sermons is the prioritization of unconditional love, the challenge to choose love over the hatred and bigotry that, to this day, disenfranchise and oppress Black Americans and people of color through racism. To avoid this context when reading and reflecting on Martin Luther King Jr.'s work would be to access his words through a privileged and ignorant lens, both passively and actively erasing historical memory and trauma from the context in which this language was spoken. We urge you to be mindful of this when reflecting on your own dreams: How do your dreams have an impact on others? In what ways do your dreams promote love and justice for all?

"The new world is a world of geographical togetherness. This means that no individual or nation can live alone. We must all learn to live together, or we will be forced to die together."

In an age of globalism
and technology, the
ability to connect with
those all over the world
has never been easier.
With this comes not
only the excitement of
connection, but also the
consideration of how our
actions have an impact
on those in and outside
of our local network.
In what ways will your
dreams influence the
communities around you?
And how might your
community aid you in
achieving your goals?

THE
Struggle

"An individual has not started living until he can rise above the narrow confines of his individualistic concerns to the broader concerns of all humanity."

Part of actualizing your dreams is learning their context, history, and urgencies regarding the world around you. What are overarching issues that you see across the world? What other topics do you want to study that you think will help you gain better footing in your goals?

THE
Power

"[They] . . . have come to realize that their destiny is tied up with our destiny. And they have come to realize that their freedom is inextricably bound to our freedom."

Our greatest strength will always be our humanity—wonderfully rich and diverse, but always unified by the realities of life and the rights we all share, though they may be exercised inequitably and unjustly. Write about times you have practiced empathy, listened to others, and tried to understand their points of view. What stories have you consumed via article, book, television, podcast, etc. about events and injustices that are happening all over the world that you care about? What passions, skills, or values that you may have written about in previous sections could you apply to making the world a better place for all those near and far? How might helping others in these ways also improve your own life? What resources would help you expand your knowledge of the causes you care about?

"If you can't fly then run, if you can't run then walk, if you can't walk then crawl, but whatever you do you have to keep moving forward."

Earlier, you reflected on what the first steps would look like for achieving your dreams, for yourself and the world. This space is also meant to acknowledge that the first steps are often difficult, and even the smallest step can be a struggle. But there is room to celebrate what you've accomplished at every stage. Here, list things you have done for yourself or others that you are proud of: this can be something like eating a meal, calling a friend, emailing a contact, volunteering for an hour. No matter how small they may seem, how inconsequential you believe them to be, they are still something. And something, no matter what anybody tells you, is a wondrous and courageous thing.

THE
Path

"And I say to you,
I have also decided to
stick to love. For I know
that love is ultimately
the only answer to
mankind's problems."

In a sermon, Martin Luther King Jr. said
something of a similar vein, stating that "I have
decided to stick with love. Hate is too great a
burden to bear." In Part I, you thought about
limitations, what or who has made you feel
like your dreams must be deferred. It is valid,
yes, to initially feel antagonism, frustration,
confusion, and anger toward these blocks. It
is also incredibly valid after these exercises
to struggle with choosing love over hatred,
choosing forgiveness over bitterness.

Why do you feel these
factors have been
impeding your growth?

How do you want
to reframe these
relationships to feel
more safe, secure, and
self-actualized?

In what ways can you redefine or expand your definitions of love to live a more fulfilling life and invest in the causes you believe in?

Having reflected on self-love, communal love, and unconditional love, how do you wish to apply love to your own dreams? What are ways in which you can instill love in your daily and long-term actions?

Furthermore, now is a good time to take stock of the questions and answers that you've considered during your engagement with, and creation of, this journal.

1. Reread what you've written under the section "The Dream" for personal and social transformation. Write about what you notice that's similar or different.

2. Reread what you've
   written under the
   section "The Struggle"
   for personal and
   social transformation.
   Write about what you
   notice that's similar or
   different.

3. Reread what you've
   written under the
   section "The Power"
   for personal and
   social transformation.
   Write about what you
   notice that's similar
   or different.

4. Reread what you've
   written under the
   section "The Path"
   for personal and
   social transformation.
   Write about what you
   notice that's similar or
   different.

5. Write about what you now realize connects personal and social transformation for you.

6. In what ways can
   what you now know
   about personal
   transformation affect
   the actions you take for
   social transformation?
   And how can what
   you now know about
   social transformation
   affect your personal
   transformation?

The goal of this reflection is not to blame yourself
for your current emotions or feel guilt for holding
negativity, but to acknowledge your anger and
frustrations and work toward a relationship
with yourself and others that can make you feel
empowered to prioritize your own dreams and
ultimately use your skills to promote love and
kindness to those around you.

"Now is the time
to make justice a
reality for all of
God's children."

Everyone has a story, and everyone deserves justice—you, your best friend, your neighbor, and someone halfway around the world whom you've never met and may never know. Often, stories, dreams, and quests for justice overlap and intersect in ways you may not realize at first. In what ways do your dreams for yourself and your community intersect, connect with the past, and work toward a better present and future? If you were to push yourself toward achieving your dreams, accepting the challenges you will face armed with the resources you have identified, what would you do today? What would you do tomorrow? Next week? Next month? A path is built by taking one step at a time. Step by step, you will walk your path.

"So I say to you, my friends, that even though we must face the difficulties of today and tomorrow, I still have a dream."

It is helpful to return to the quote that began this journal. Now, after having taken the time to think about your values, your goals, your community, the needs and injustices you see in the world, and your capacity to move forward with love, return to the first journal entry.

Reread your dreams from each section. In this space, validate your dreams and the agency you have to achieve whatever you set your mind to. Like Toni Morrison once said, you are your own best thing. How would you like to continue this journey forward?